Remembering

The St. Louis WORLD'S FAIR

The Louisiana Purchase Monument.

Remembering
The St. Louis WORLD'S FAIR

Text...
MARGARET JOHANSON WITHERSPOON

Pen and Ink Drawings...
FRANCES JOHANSON KREBS FAIN

Photography...
ELINOR MARTINEAU COYLE

Book designed by Francis J. Krebs Fain and Elinor M. Coyle

COVER
Festival Hall, Colonnade of States and Grand Basin.

COMFORT PRINTING CO.
1611 LOCUST ST.
ST. LOUIS, MISSOURI 63103

Library of Congress Catalog Card Number 73-83070

Printed in the United States of America

To all St. Louisans—of Yesterday, of Today, of Tomorrow—in whose hearts may dwell pride and esteem of this radiant community; and especially to the memory of the respected gentlemen who so untiringly made possible the wondrous St. Louis Fair of 1904, this book is dedicated.

Waiting for the parade.

Acknowledgements

The writing of this book has been, for me, a most enjoyable excursion into a hitherto unexplored age of splendor. It would not have been possible without the patience and cooperation of the librarians of the Missouri Historical Society and the St. Louis Public Library, who so efficiently assisted me in my research.

I also want to express my appreciation to all those who so graciously responded to my quests, often supplying me with pictures and maps, as well as valuable information.

Especially am I deeply indebted to all the members of my family who so enthusiastically and whole-heartedly supported me in this venture.

Photograph page 11, courtesy Sheraton-Jefferson Hotel.

Photographs page 18, courtesy Wanamaker's.

Insert—A folded transparent overlay map
of the Fair Grounds area in 1973.

TABLE OF CONTENTS

*Crumbling wall along
Forest Park Expressway.*

Foreword

 ERTAINLY I am only one among thousands whose parents or grand-parents have delighted them with descriptions of the St. Louis World's Fair of 1904. But just how many of these thousands are aware that there are many remnants of that Fair still to be seen in and around St. Louis?

The crumbling concrete wall along the Forest Park Expressway has figured in my life almost daily since childhood, but when I learned that it was built to form the northern boundary of the Fair Grounds, it took on a new and sentimental aura. I found myself wishing that it could be preserved and stories of the Fair woven again around its timeworn mortar.

Why this sentimentality about an old wall? Perhaps a growing appreciation of the yesterdays of St. Louis; perhaps the reminiscing of stories told by parents long gone from the scene; perhaps a desire, along with other St. Louisans, to preserve the valued old things in this age of the bull-dozer.

What else was there for me to see that would recall those golden days and bring back visions of the splendor of this Fair? Are there others who would share my interest and curiosity? Is it possible that many St. Louisans, standing at the threshold of the diamond jubilee of that great Fair, might also want to re-live its moments?

These questions drove me to the libraries where I discovered such a wealth of material that I became hopelessly absorbed in re-living those exciting days. Gradually realizing that the unfolding drama of the Fair was equally as captivating as a search for its relics, I became convinced that its story had a charming appeal. Inasmuch as no book describing it had been brought forth since the early years of the century, it seemed reasonable to suppose that St. Louisans, now so keenly interested in protecting and preserving the city's grand old showplaces, would welcome a brief recounting of the world's largest exposition—The Universal Exposition of 1904! Hence this small volume, which I hope will whet your appetite for further exploration into an age of never-to-be-forgotten St. Louis history.

Margaret Johanson Witherspoon

Fair strollers.

Beginnings

AT THE turn of the twentieth century St. Louis was a thriving city—fourth in population in the nation. Its remarkable growth from a frontier town during the first half of the nineteenth century was largely due to the westward expansion of the nation and the burgeoning traffic on the Mississippi River. Civic-minded business men, hoping to reinforce the city's development, wanted to attract one of the many expositions being promoted in the latter part of the century. The Columbian Exposition of 1893 had loomed invitingly, but unfortunately the city was poorly equipped with adequate hotel facilities and so this prize went to Chicago. Energetic construction followed with the hope that the hundredth anniversary celebration of the Louisiana Purchase might become the 1903 International Exposition held in St. Louis.

Every effort was bent toward developing the interest of the populace and enlisting the cooperation of the fourteen states and territories comprising the Louisiana Purchase area. St. Louis agreed to raise ten million dollars and the states agreed to support all efforts to obtain a grant from Congress for five million dollars. Action by Congress was sought in February, 1899, but it took two sessions of this body, much travel to Washington, many delays, dissensions and concessions (one of these was that the Fair remain closed on Sundays) before the bill finally became law—just *thirty minutes* before the close of the Fifty-sixth Congress in March, 1901. The strain of the final forty-eight hours was so intense that instead of the customary congratulatory hand-shakes, the triumphant workers greeted each other with emotional embraces.

Immediately the Louisiana Purchase Exposition Company was formed, David R. Francis was elected president, stock was sold and the Fair was rolling.

Enthusiasm ran high as St. Louisans watched the Jefferson Hotel rise above Twelfth Boulevard. Much other construction followed. The West End felt the boom. In 1903, ninety-four established hotels were in operation and by the opening date of April 30, 1904, fifteen more were ready.

The site chosen for the Fair was the western half of Forest Park. The city had acquired this park in 1874 after much contention. Many voices had been raised in objection: "we already have several good parks"; "it will be the rich man's park—the poor can never get there"; "the city will never grow that far west!" By the 1890's this impossible park was serving the city in a variety of exciting ways: "Boating and skating on its natural lakes, drives through its wooded areas, activities at the Hippodrome (a large recreational harness-racing track located west of the DeBaliviere entrance and the scene of weekly events sponsored by the Gentlemen's Riding Club), dining in "The Cottage"—THE place for elegant banquets—and even opportunities to view a few donated zoo specimens.

Jefferson Hotel still standing at Twelfth and Locust.

Business men of the Carondelet area were visibly disturbed. They had made a strong bid to draw the Fair to the south side. "It is a 'natural'," they said, "bluffs on the river, beautiful rocky terrain, railroads nearby, and the grand sweep of the Mississippi, unmarred by bridges, buildings, levees and commerce. How could any committee select a site without a grand waterway?" Their forceful pleas failed in favor of Forest Park with its small but natural Peninsular Lake.

The chosen area covered about 650 acres but it soon became evident that much more space would be needed for the type of exposition planned. Additional tracts were obtained by lease—the new, yet unoccupied Washington University campus with seven completed buildings and four more destined for completion by Opening Day, and other private lands nearby. The resulting area comprised about 1275 acres. By contrast, the four largest expositions this nation had known all together covered only 1319 acres. (These were: the Centennial at Philadelphia in 1876, the Columbian at Chicago in 1893, the Trans-Mississippi at Omaha in 1898 and the Pan-American at Buffalo in 1901.)

The intent of this exposition was early defined and it carried a new note: *Life* and *Movement* would be its distinguishing marks. It would be an exhibition of *Man* as well as his *Works;* it would be *processes* as well as *products,* in contrast to former fairs that had specialized mainly in finished articles.

Preparations for the Fair consumed several years, the early ones being concerned with arousing the interest of the nation and foreign states; the later ones with the actual physical work—which was being pushed to the limit for a 1903 opening. Preparations became daily more frenzied and soon it was apparent that to attempt to open in 1903 would be disastrous. Postponement was needed and the city sighed with relief when Congress granted the request for a year's delay to 1904. This action allowed President Francis to obtain many more foreign exhibits and encouraged more national business corporations to plan displays.

Matchless Man

David R. Francis on Opening Day.

WORDS are lacking to describe the man who was the moving force behind the Fair—David Rowland Francis. Former Mayor of St. Louis, former Governor of Missouri and former Cabinet Secretary, Mr. Francis was endowed with a singular vision, an enthusiasm and an untiring energy seldom granted to one individual. He had a charming cordiality of manner and the kind of magnetism which makes natural leaders. In addition, he was surrounded by men of equally high calibre. His board officers included William H. Thompson, Walter B. Stevens, James L. Blair, Franklin Ferriss, Corwin H. Spencer, Samuel M. Kennard, Daniel M. Houser, Cyrus P. Walbridge, Seth W. Cobb, Charles H. Huttig, August Gehner and Pierre Chouteau, a descendant of the founding family of St. Louis. Rolla Wells was the Mayor of the city. This strong coalition of dedicated men was instrumental in making the St. Louis Fair the largest and finest of all time.

The prodigious work, the travels and maneuvers of President Francis would challenge the most competent public servant even in this age of air travel, and to read of his activities and movements leaves one breathless. His whirlwind tour of Europe in nineteen days was highly successful even though doubters had predicted doom. A newspaper cartoon of the day pictured this amazing man standing, reins in hands, with one foot on a speeding locomotive, the other on a huge steamship plowing through the waves. To him *should* go all the accolades that were accorded him during the Fair—gifts from foreign states, grateful recognition by the city, and a governor-decreed "D. R. Francis Day" complete with parade and elaborate festivities.

As if these accomplishments were not enough, this extraordinary man, in the years following the Fair, published a large two-volume work completely describing every minute aspect of it, with columns of figures and financial statements that would answer any query concerning its operations. Furthermore, he was instrumental in securing for the people of St. Louis a lasting memento of the exposition— the Jefferson Memorial Building.

Gavel used by David R. Francis at Opening Day ceremony, now at Jefferson Memorial.

Splendid Achievement

MUCH work had to be done to make the chosen location as desirable as the grandeur of the Fair demanded. First, Peninsular Lake, located below the present Art Hill, had to be re-shaped; its bounds were irregular and it had a few islands in it. Also, running through Forest Park on a winding course was a little river—the River Des Peres— spoken of in a Park Commissioner's Report as being navigable! Since this river was prone to flood occasionally, one of the first conquests had to be its control. By boxing it in and changing its course to remove it from unwanted areas, the nearby hillside and the re-designed Peninsular Lake were ready for further development. This lake, with a new name—The Grand Basin— was connected by lagoons with other lakes, providing a never-ending panoramic view. It was a remarkable engineering and designing feat to make of these simple, natural waterways a scene grand enough to meet the high qualifications of the planners.

William H. Thompson driving the first stake, September 3, 1901.

Ceremonies - - Ceremonies

T HE Exposition was rich in ceremony, the first of which occurred on September 3, 1901, with the driving of the first stake, located 300 feet southwest of the future Sculpture Hall. Made from a young oak on the grounds, highly polished and varnished, the stake served as the architectural radiating center of the Fair layout. Ironically, the elaborately-planned service was delayed some time because President Francis failed to arrive. A search party found the carriage with its important passengers wandering through "The Wilderness"—a densely-thicketed forest in the northwest corner of Forest Park—lost!

About three months later, on December 20, 1901, during an unusually cold St. Louis winter, the Ground-breaking Ceremony took place. With five inches of snow on the ground and a temperature of ten degrees below zero, a large log heap was kept burning at the site (which was a little southwest of today's Jefferson Memorial) to thaw the ground. Three shovels, each of historical significance, were used for the digging at this spot, where the statue of St. Louis would be placed.

Shovel used for ground-breaking.

14

Because the Fair had been postponed, a Day of Dedication was in order, and this was held on April 30, 1903. Witnessed by some 350,000 persons lining the streets to watch the processional, it was one of the most elaborate dedications of that era. President Theodore Roosevelt, Ex-president Grover Cleveland and Mayor Rolla Wells greeted the 50,000 persons which President Francis estimated crowded into the Palace of Liberal Arts to participate in the ceremony. Lavish press reports of the event gave such an impetus to the exposition that hundreds of requests poured in for exhibit space.

President Francis touching the key to open the Exposition.

The work of another year wrought the magic of completion. But the spring was cold in St. Louis and on April 20, 1904, a heavy snow storm slowed all operations. Anxiety prevailed in the final rush to complete the job. However, when Opening Day, April 30, 1904, dawned fair and crisp, everything was in readiness for the grand celebration, until then unequalled in the history of world's fairs.

Conducted in the Plaza of St. Louis, the Opening Day ceremony included prayer and music as well as speeches. John Phillip Sousa led his band and a chorus of four hundred voices in the rendition of Stedman's "Hymn of the West," written expressly for the occasion. William H. Taft,

"Open ye gates! Swing wide ye portals! Enter herein ye sons of men. Learn the lessons here taught and gather from it inspiration for still greater accomplishments!"
—David R. Francis   April 30, 1904

United States Secretary of War, made the principal address, and Mr. Francis touched a telegraph key which would alert President Theodore Roosevelt in Washington. Then pressing his telegraph key, the President of the United States formally opened the Fair, at which moment ten thousand flags suddenly fluttered from their masts; fountains shot geysers and spray; cascades splashed down the hillsides. The statue of St. Louis watched over the proceedings, extending the city's welcome to all, symbolically flanked by DeSoto and Joliet, early explorers of the Mississippi area.

Example of ornate work.

Fair Design

UTILIZING the sweeping hillside above the newly-designed lake, the Fair's architects planned to capitalize on this favorable topography as the center of interest. The natural semi-circular hill, now known as Art Hill, was crowned with Festival Hall, and flanked on each side of it, connected by stately colonnades, was a lesser pavilion. Festival Hall housed the huge auditorium; the latter two, restaurants. From each of these three, a large cascade of sparkling water flowed down the hill into the Grand Basin.

Alongside the cascades were great staircases ornately decorated with statuary, benches and landscaped gardens. At night the cascades were lighted in softly-changing colors—a triumph of this emerging age of electricity—cleverly achieved by the installation of triple wiring and sockets, with automatic dimming effects. The change from one color to the next, barely perceptible, was awe-inspiring to the visitors.

Festival Hall at the top of Art Hill commanded a position of prominence, its dome larger than that of St. Peter's in Rome. The two smaller pavilions flanking it were called "The Atlantic" and "The Pacific," expressing a symbolism of the vastness of the United States' domain.

Festival Hall at night.

Liberal Arts Palace.

17

Festival Hall's auditorium seated three thousand persons, and its stage housed the largest pipe organ ever built—with five manuals and one hundred forty stops. Built in Los Angeles by The Art Organ Company, it required ten railroad cars to transport it to its site. St. Louis' Charles Galloway, then only thirty-two years old, played host to many world-famous organists in his position as official organist. At the close of the Fair the organ was stored for several years, then purchased by Wanamaker's and rebuilt in their Philadelphia store. First played there in 1911, it is even now played three times daily for the enjoyment of shoppers.

*Close-up of Eagle
from German Exhibit.*

Wanamaker's. whose trade mark is the eagle, also acquired from the Fair the unusual bronze eagle—which was the gift of the Kaiser—displayed in the German Exhibit. Wrought in bronze by August Gaul of Berlin, this eagle was the first of its kind, although a similar one had been made of cast iron for the 1900 Paris Exposition. It was entirely worked by hand. On the head alone were 1600 bronze feathers and the overall total was 5000, each of which was hammered and bent by hand while hot.

The Colonnade of States, linking Festival Hall and the Pavilions, was graced with giant seated figures, seven on each side, each representing a state or territory of the Louisiana Purchase. (These were: Louisiana, Arkansas, Missouri, Iowa, Minnesota, North Dakota, South Dakota, Nebraska, Kansas, Oklahoma, Montana, Wyoming, Colorado, and Indian Territory.) The sculptors of these figures were all young men of promise who had not yet achieved reputations in their field.

Eight exhibition palaces, ornate with Victorian opulence, surrounded the Grand Basin. (They were: Mines and Metallurgy, Liberal Arts, Education and Social Economy, Manufactures, Electricity, Varied Industries, Transportation, and Machinery.) Each was different in design, yet each conformed to certain standards in order to create pleasing effects as well as to establish safety factors. For example: each building must have a specified height for the roofline; all windows must open; every building must have entrances on all sides; color was permitted only on roofs, towers and minor decorations. Massive in size, each palace covered several acres. The largest one—Transportation—covered fifteen acres (nine football fields)!

Although the buildings were ornate and appeared to be very substantial, they were made of temporary materials, not to last more than a few years. The material employed was "staff," first used at the Paris Exposition of 1878 and again at the Columbian Fair in Chicago in 1893. This firm but temporary substance was a mixture of fibres soaked in simple plaster-of-paris. The resulting hardened material was very adaptable. It could be sawed, hammered, nailed and whittled like wood. Originally burlap was used as the binder at twelve cents a pound; but later, discovery of the use of manila fibres at four cents a pound allowed architectural imaginations to run wild. By pouring "staff" into glue molds, many repeated ornamental effects could be achieved in a very short time.

The basic structure under the "staff" could be wood or steel. For the St. Louis Fair, the long-leafed yellow pine (ninety-million feet of it) was given preference over steel for several reasons, the most important being the impossibility of obtaining sufficient steel in time.

Another development was the "pointing machine"—a three-dimensional enlarger made on the same principle as the two-dimensional one known as the pantograph. These improvements made possible the rich rococo effects of the palaces. In studios all over the country sculptors were at work under contract on the scale models assigned to them to execute. Made in clay one-fourth their final size, they were then cast in plaster-of-paris and sent to an enlarging studio. Professional sculptors later added refining touches.

Behind Festival Hall stood a permanent structure—the Art Palace. This building would house the valuable art objects lent to the Fair by twenty nations. To allow for as large a display as possible, two temporary buildings flanked the Art Palace east and west, and a smaller annex, the Sculpture Pavilion, was on the south—thus forming an attractive courtyard. The temporary structures were removed after the Fair and the Art Palace, donated to the city of St. Louis by the Exposition Company, is now the present St. Louis Art Museum.

St. Louis Art Museum today.

Inviting waterways flowed between many of the large exhibition palaces, but in some places there were broad plazas and dignified landscaped gardens graced with allegorical and symbolic statues. Of special interest and widely admired was a luxuriant sunken garden located between the Liberal Arts Palace and the Mines and Metallurgy Palace. Cleverly capitalizing on the available topography, the landscape architect built this garden on the site of a former lake which had been known since 1893 as the Post-Dispatch Lake.

The origin of this lake is an interesting story of community cooperation. During the depression of 1893, the Post-Dispatch newspaper promoted a campaign to provide jobs for many men in the city who were suffering unemployment. A subscription list was opened by the newspaper and, together with the $20,000 contributed by the Lindell Railway, $40,000 was raised which provided work for many men—namely, to dig an extension of Peninsular Lake in Forest Park. Women volunteers each day cooked hot noon meals for the men, and by 1894 the project was completed, forming what is now the boating lake and called "Post-Dispatch Lake."

At the time of the Fair this lake had to be drained and partially filled to make way for the two palaces—*and* the sunken garden. When the park was re-designed after the Fair, the lake was again dug out and restored to its former condition. Since that time boating, fishing and ice-skating have been popular attractions on Post-Dispatch Lake.

Sunken Garden located between Liberal Arts and Mines and Metallurgy Palaces (present location now a part of Post-Dispatch Lake).

States at Home

HE area occupied today by the St. Louis Zoo grounds was the Plateau of States, where many states erected large houses which served as gathering places for visitors. Some of these buildings were replicas of important historical places, such as The Cabildo of Louisiana (the place of the Louisiana Purchase transaction), Tennessee's Hermitage, Virginia's Monticello and Mississippi's Beauvoir. Other state buildings were quite simple, representing the early pioneer life of the state. Some were enormous and some were so unusual as to command a second look. One such was the "Wigwam," home of the State of Washington. This captivating structure, nine stories tall, was built octagonally by the use of eight ninety-foot timbers which tapered to a cupola at the top. An elevator took visitors to the apex to see a superb view of the Fair. The lengthy timbers rest today in a St. Louis County lumber yard stacked with seasoning lumber.

For its home, the State of Maine built a hunting lodge made of native logs, assembled without benefit of nails. At the close of the Fair it was sold to a group of hunters who moved it to the Ozarks for their lodge. Later it became the first building of the now well-known School of the Ozarks at Hollister, Missouri. Many who have visited the Shepherd-of-the-Hills country remember this old log building which, unfortunately, was destroyed by fire in the 1940's.

"The Wigwam"—State of Washington Building.

*State of Maine Building, "a club house of the woods"—later Dobyns Hall at the
School of the Ozarks, Hollister, Missouri.*

Nevada House.

*New Hampshire House. Both houses, somewhat
altered, are in the St. Louis area today.*

The Missouri Building.

Missouri, the host state, constructed a building made entirely of native materials. Designed as a permanent building, its dome was reminiscent of a state capitol building. Not only was it large and handsome, but it also boasted a cooling system as well as a heating system—for at that time St. Louis summers had a reputation! On November 19—just two weeks before the close of the Fair—the building and almost all of its contents were destroyed by fire. However, a set of formal French gilded furniture—one of the few items rescued—may still be seen in the drawing room of the Executive Mansion in Jefferson City. Naturally, no attempt was made to replace the expensive building at such a late date.

Gilt chairs at Governor's Mansion, rescued from the fire.

The World's Fair Pavilion, built near the site of the Missouri Building.

Detail of the arches.

However, after the Fair, a pavilion—a gift of the Exposition Company to the City of St. Louis—was erected near the place to memorialize the Fair. Because it has been known through the years as the World's Fair Pavilion, many persons mistakenly believe it to be a remnant of the Fair itself.

On the hillside just below the Missouri Building stood the massive United States Government Building, constructed of steel and the largest exposition edifice ever erected by the Government up to that time.

Close by, the U. S. Fisheries Building was a constant attraction with its forty glass-fronted fish tanks and a center pool for seals. On this hill today, a colored fountain and landscaped gardens provide an attraction for park visitors.

Located in the same vicinity, the Bird Cage, a unique structure and the largest of its kind ever built, was the exhibition of the Smithsonian Institution. It, too, was left to the city after the Fair. It has recently been renovated after having undergone some alterations over the years, and once again sightseers may actually walk through the giant cage.

Watching the aquatic animals in the United States Government Fisheries Building.

Near the Plateau of States was another temporary structure called The Inside Inn. It was the only hotel within the Fair Grounds. A large rambling building constructed on a hillside, it had 2257 rooms and could take care of 5500 persons. Located just inside the southern boundary of Forest Park, its site now yields to the frenzied traffic of the Daniel Boone Expressway at Hampton Avenue (U.S. 40). The idea of providing a hotel within the grounds originated with an E. M. Statler of Buffalo, New York, and from this auspicious and successful beginning his famous chain of hotels was developed.

Bird Cage after renovation.

F. JOHANSON KREBS

THE Place

THE GRAND BASIN was the focal point for all the important activities. Boat parades celebrating various events were held almost daily. Boats were also an inviting way for sightseers to view the main features of the Fair, as the lagoons and waterways flowed between the exhibition buildings. North of the Grand Basin, the Plaza of St. Louis—with its tall Louisiana Purchase Monument and Statue of St. Louis—was the scene of all the official proceedings.

Crossing this plaza lay the Louisiana Way, main thoroughfare of the Fair Grounds and stretching symbolically from France's palace, the Grand Trianon, on the west to the United States Government Building on the east—the two nations involved in the Louisiana Purchase transaction. Along this avenue traversed all the official parades of the Fair.

The Louisiana Purchase Monument.

Palace of France—modelled after the Grand Trianon at Versailles.

Nature at Work

THE long gentle hill lying just west of Forest Park provided a space large enough for agricultural exhibitions and the largest building on the Fair Grounds—the Agriculture Palace, with its eastern facade one-third of a mile long! Even so, space was lacking and many of the exhibits were set up on the lawns outside where there were demonstration plots of various types of grasses, pools with water plants, and a charming windmill village displaying numerous types of mills all whirring away with the slightest breeze.

Nearby was the Horticulture Palace and also a livestock area with daily shows, judgings and awards.

Near the northern entrance of the Agriculture Palace, a giant floral clock lay on a hillside, the largest time-piece ever built. Its dial, 112 feet in diameter, was a bed of neatly trimmed flowers and foliage with 12-foot long numbers in contrasting foliage. The giant hands, weighing 2500 pounds, were operated by compressed air controlled by a master clock in a miniature pavilion located at the "twelve." On one side of this pavilion, a smaller building housed the bell, and on the other side, a big hour-glass filled with one hundred pounds of sand turned automatically on each hour.

The giant Floral Clock.

30

Windmill Hill.

"Hour Gardens" surrounded the dial: plants that opened at certain hours of the day so that there was a continuous hourly florescence from 6:00 A.M. to 6:00 P.M. throughout the summer. At the moment of striking the hour and half-hour, the pavilion doors opened automatically to reveal the clock mechanism at work, then closed at the end of the tolling. Brilliantly illuminated at night with one thousand lights hidden in the foliage, and booming the hour and half-hour with a bell that resounded over most of the Grounds, this ingenious floral time-piece was one of the Fair's great attractions.

*Gargoyle decorations
on Brookings Hall.*

Modern Model Campus

WASHINGTON UNIVERSITY'S newly-developing campus was not only valuable in providing needed space for the Fair's Administration but it also served as an exhibit of a model university. The Administration Building (Brookings Hall) was the place of all the official meetings and reception of guests. Other buildings furnished space for exhibits, offices and meeting rooms. At the western end of the campus, the imposing athletic field and gymnasium, in use today by the University, was the location of an elaborate physical culture program, as well as the Olympic Games of 1904.

Administration Building (the present Brookings Hall) and Villa of Italy.

Brookings Hall today.

Francis Field today.
Physical Education
Building is seen
in the background.

Foreign states—China, Sweden, Brazil and others—were grouped at the eastern end. Notable among these was the handsome British Building, a copy of Queen Anne's Orangery at Kensington Gardens, originally designed by Christopher Wren early in the eighteenth century. (An orangery is a place to grow oranges!) Interesting for its majestic simplicity, unusual formal gardens and also because it was purchased by the University at the close of the Fair, it served for many years as the home of its School of Fine Arts. The interior was designed to display period rooms from British history: there was an Elizabethan Room, a Queen Anne's Room, a Georgian Room and a faithful reproduction of the banquet hall in Kensington Palace. Ornate plaster moldings adorned the ceilings and beautiful dark wainscotings and fireplaces enhanced the interiors. Many St. Louisans remember attending not only University art classes but also children's Saturday art classes in this temporary building, which over the years became sadly rundown.

Copy of ceiling of banquet hall from Kensington Palace (Bixby Hall).

Not until 1926 did the School of Fine Arts abandon the Orangery for the new Bixby Hall at the corner of Forsyth and Skinker. Since the Orangery interiors were of permanent materials, many of them were retained for the new building and may be seen in the Director's office and the Great Hall of Bixby Hall.

Sixteenth Century Tudor mantel in Elizabethan Room of Orangery—now in director's office of School of Fine Arts (Bixby Hall).

Detail of carving on Tudor mantel.

The Orangery—Great Britain's Palace.

F. JOHANSON KREBS

Primitives

ERHAPS the most commanding of all the exhibits at the Fair was the Philippines' stockade. Largest and most costly of all the foreign exhibits (two million dollars), it was instrumental in bringing 1100 Filipinos to live for seven months in this country. Arrowhead Lake, a natural lake lying along today's Wydown and DeMun Avenues, provided a perfect setting in a rolling wooded area of forty-seven acres. Around this lake were set up communities of various aboriginal tribes—Moros, Visayans, Igorots, Negritos and many others. Each tribe constructed its own village—some were huts on stilts above water, others were thatched huts on the hillside—and each tribe exhibited its primitive life and culture.

The people came in droves to view the Primitive Villages.

Many Fair visitors, when asked about the most impressive exhibit of the Exposition, named this one. Americans were seeing for the first time representatives of primitive peoples and their strange cultures. At no previous exposition had such a large and interesting array of rarely-seen tribes been gathered. Visitors were fascinated with observing an unusual tribal wedding ceremony, and also viewing a new-born Igorot baby, born in the compound during the Fair. One scantily-clothed chieftain created a scene by refusing to permit his tribe to be viewed until a telephone had been installed in his hut!

Stylish ladies on way to view naked savages.

And the Igorots caused havoc with their demand for dogs, the main staple in their native diet. The Humane Society and dog-lovers all over the city rose in mighty indignation and newspapers aired the heated contest in daily articles. In the end it must have been begrudgingly settled in some fashion as the tribe was here—and remained here—and its people had to be fed! Following the Fair and the return of these natives to their homeland, Arrowhead Lake was drained, filled and used for land development and park areas.

Scene from a Moro Village. The Moros' ruler was represented at the Exposition by his Prime Minister whose name was Datto Fecundi. The Datto is shown standing in his doorway. A bamboo bridge leads to his house which was built over the water of Arrowhead Lake. In his home were what appeared to be brass kettles inverted and arranged in a row. These were really musical instruments so constructed as to produce a variety of tones. The Moro girls beat on these instruments with heavy sticks, producing music which had melody but, of course, was monotonous.

Floral Map

The Floral Map.

 OT far from the compound of the Primitives and a little north of Wydown, a floral map of the United States was spread out on a broad meadow. Its scale was one inch to the mile and it was positioned in its correct north/south orientation. State lines were outlined by narrow gravel pathways and in each state's plot were planted vegetation and flowers indigenous to that state. Plants of the warmer climates were forced under glass during the winter months so that on Opening Day each state had flowers and mature vegetation on display.

World's Fair Mural in University City Post Office.

40

Entrancing Entrances

TEN different entrance gates and a fee of fifty cents admitted a person to the Fair. The new automatic turnstiles evoked surprise as well as praise. Until the correct coin was inserted, the gate would not open! Hardly newsworthy in today's world, this innovation delighted visitors and attendants alike, as the Chicago Fair had suffered many difficulties because of bungling at the gates. Once inside the Grounds, the sightseer sought out the Intramural Railway—an electric streetcar line operating only within the Grounds and designed expressly for transporting visitors over the area. Its route covered all the important exhibition sites with seventeen stations on its circuit.

Intramural Railroad, at Skinker and Wydown.

Ways of Travel

ONCE a fairgoer had reached his destination—by city streetcars, local train from Union Station or even in one of the ten tallyho automobiles which carried twenty or more passengers—there were many methods of transportation within the Grounds. In addition to the Intramural Railway and three miniature trains, boats of all kinds plied the lakes and lagoons—gondolas with singing gondoliers, electric launches, dragon-shaped boats, steam launches—in which sightseers could catch a panoramic view of the main buildings. Automobiles were available for hire, also roller chairs, jinrickshas, and zebu carriages. For the more daring there were camel, burro and elephant rides.

Although there had been no automobiles at the Columbian Fair eleven years before, quite a few St. Louisans owned these new-fangled horseless carriages in 1904, some even equipped with "wireless" poles to pick up messages being sent daily from the DeForest Wireless Tower. Quite incredible was the "great parade of autos on August 12th that had started from the Atlantic seaboard cities and had come to St. Louis (via Chicago) in a constantly increasing procession." There were one hundred twenty-two of these cars of every make and style. Weeks of driving, tire-changing and do-it-yourself repairs over incredibly bad roads did not deter these motor-age enthusiasts from this gruelling endurance run. An impressive parade of

Gondola on the Grand Basin.

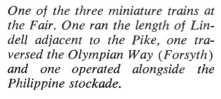

One of the three miniature trains at the Fair. One ran the length of Lindell adjacent to the Pike, one traversed the Olympian Way (Forsyth) and one operated alongside the Philippine stockade.

these automobiles, escorted from the Jefferson Hotel by St. Louis-owned cars, passed through the Exposition Grounds with their vehicles in the condition in which they had arrived. The extent of enthusiasm in this embryonic industry was evident too in the exhibition in the Transportation Palace of one hundred sixty kinds of vehicles—electric, gas and steam-propelled.

Some have actually labelled this Fair an "exposition of transportation." Although that was not the stated intent of the Exposition Committee, it is understandable, considering the size of the Transportation Palace, the fine displays of the latest in railroad equipment and the rapid expansion of the motor industry as shown by its exhibits.

The newest phase of transportation—aeronautics—was not overlooked either. The western part of the Washington University campus was home for these neophyte "bird-men." Here, eleven acres were set aside for the large balloons, and a fence thirty-feet in height was constructed to completely enclose the area. This acted as a windbreak to make handling the balloons easier. Nearby a large barn-like building was built so that they might be more conveniently filled with gas.

Various types of craft were brought for show, bearing labels all the way from airships, aeroplanes, flying machines, balloons and kites, to one called a gliding machine. With handsome prize money as a lure ($100,000) entrants were eager to display their inventions and flying talents. However, as might be expected, most flights were of short duration, ended unsuccessfully or even drastically, due to faulty equipment, poor design or inadequate preparation. The aeronautic age was still in its infancy and it would be about another six years before air travel would begin to take its place in the family of man.

Zebu carriage—another mode of transportation. Note ornate decorations.

The Pike

THE PIKE, an inviting one-mile stretch along the northern edge of the Fair Grounds, captivated all. Like a giant amusement park, its center avenue was lined on each side with beckoning concessions. Sightseers very often carried an ice cream cone, for the Pike was the birthplace of this savory delight. And it was an instant success. Going to the Fair was not complete without a taste of its wonderful sweetness.

The forerunner of the popsickle was here too. Called "fruit icicles," these summer thirst-quenchers were made of fruit juices frozen in narrow tin tubes; the warmth of the hand allowed the icicle to slip slowly from the tube for easy and refreshing sipping.

Another "first" at the Fair was iced tea. Its invention is an intriguing tale: A tea house was having an extremely hard time selling hot tea on summer days until an unsung hero thought to pour it over crushed ice. The tea house manager immediately picked up this clever idea. And sales sky-rock-

F. JOHANSON KREBS

eted! Thus "iced tea"—a boon to mankind ever since—was introduced to the world. The claim that the first "hot dog" was served on the Pike also seems to be well justified. (Could the Igorots have had an influence on this name?)

At the eastern end of the Pike, the massive Tyrolean Alps hovered over a storybook Swiss village below. Here amusement seekers could take a train ride into the mountains, then descend to a delicious repast in the great hall below, where many official banquets were held. (So obsessed was this age with its new-found plaything—electricity—that the huge hanging lights in this elegant hall were called "electroliers"!)

A heritage
from the Fair.

President Roosevelt was honored here at a banquet during his official visit to the Fair. Most of the St. Louis brewers were among the promoters of this concession and Adolphus Busch was its vice-president.

The Irish Village adjacent to the Alps attracted many with its medieval buildings and Celtic charm. A model of the old Irish House of Parliament lured visitors to the cafe within, and nearby Blarney Castle, housing a theatre and players, was a continual success. An extensive Industrial Hall displayed a wide variety of products which was a revelation to all and proof that Ireland was more than linens and potatoes. Here a young, little-known Irish tenor could be heard singing melodic Irish songs—his name, John McCormack.

The Pike was not only fun and frivolity, but much could be learned here too. Hagenbeck's Animal Paradise attracted large crowds who were delighted, yet apprehensive, over the bears displayed in open pits much like those in a contemporary zoo. A visit to the Baby Incubators showed the newest developments in infant care; during the Fair many premature babies were cared for on the Pike in these new life-saving devices. All types of cultures could be encountered, as numerous concessions were foreign—Fair Japan, Ancient Rome, a Chinese Village, a French Village and others.

And one could see the Galveston Flood, take a trip to the North Pole, cross the Siberian wastes on a simulated train ride, talk to the Educated Horse, witness Creation or try out the Hereafter, and watch a little-known comedian-cowboy named Will Rogers. There were rides—The Magic Whirlpool, the Water Chutes, and—as always at Fairs—the screaming Scenic Railway.

"Meet Me in St. Louie, Louie" was heard all up and down the Pike as the concessions poured forth their music with small bands and singers. The Pike was a magnet for the "ragtime" composers of the day since "ragtime" had had its origin in St. Louis. Scott Joplin, whose works are enjoying a revival as this is written seventy years later, was here and wrote "Cascade Rag" in honor of the Fair. Some other rags written at this time were "On the Pike" and "Strolling Down the Pike."

*Looking east on
Administration Avenue.*

Ferris Wheel

NEAR the Forsyth entrance the immense Observation Wheel loomed as large as a twenty-five story building. Two hundred fifty-feet high, this amazing brain-child of Mr. George Washington Gale Ferris, an engineer of Chicago, was first used at the Chicago Fair. The idea for this wheel was conceived at an afternoon club dinner, and on the moment, he fixed on the size, construction, design and even the admission fee. These details, instantly recorded on paper, were never altered! Intent that his wheel should be safe, he made the axle six times as stout as needed—the largest piece of steel ever forged up to that time and weighing seventy tons. Raising it to its position one hundred forty-feet above the ground was an engineering feat in itself. The Ferris Wheel carried thirty-six cars, each car seating sixty persons, and its movement was gentle and nearly noiseless.

F. JOHANSON KREBS

The King of Ferris Wheels.

The Wheel had been so successful at the Chicago Fair that it completely paid for itself within 4 months (original cost $380,000). One hundred and seventy-five freight cars brought the dismantled giant to St. Louis where it was rebuilt at a cost of $150,000 and served to thrill St. Louis Fair visitors.

As if this was not an amazing exhibition in itself, dare-devils used the great Wheel to display their own exhibitionism. News accounts of the day include these stories: "In one of the most unique weddings of the many which eccentric folk have had since the opening of the Exposition, a couple was married while mounted on white-spotted cow-ponies in one of the cars of the Ferris Wheel with the car at the topmost point of the Wheel." And again, "Standing on top of one of the cars of the Observation Wheel, Mrs. Maud Nicholson made the perilous trip around the Wheel Tuesday afternoon, July 12. She accomplished the same feat at the Chicago Day celebration of the World's Fair in 1893."

Since each car on the giant Ferris Wheel could seat sixty persons, it is not surprising that some imaginative person should dream up a banquet. And so it was that on a summer evening a certain gentleman was honored with such a celebration in Car No. 19 which was artistically decorated for the occasion, chef on hand, and dinner served when the car reached the zenith.

If an electrical storm knocked out the power, many riders found themselves forced to remain isolated in one of these cars, some dismayingly perched at the top of the Wheel. The guard present in each car often found it necessary to calm panicky passengers.

What happened to this mammoth wheel at the end of the Fair? Coney Island had been destined for its next stop, but that plan failed to materialize. The demolition contractor found it to be a "white elephant" and so dynamited it to bits in an awesome, much-photographed episode. It was sold as scrap for $1800. In later years, workmen in Forest Park have dug up remnants found buried under the golf course near the Forsyth entrance to the park. The original Wheel was the model for all subsequent Ferris Wheels, but there has never been another of such gigantic proportions in this country.

JAPAN

Japanese Pavilion. Located east of the Observation Wheel, the Imperial Japanese Garden was Japan's official exhibition. Building materials, brought from the Far East, were fashioned into seven attractive structures surrounded by waterfalls, miniature lakes, bridges, trained dwarfed trees and pieces of outdoor sculpture. The main pavilion with its curved roofs followed a style of architecture four hundred years old. Tea houses and a Japanese bazaar also graced the hillside. The two stone lanterns were purchased by Leonard Matthews, staunch friend of Henry Shaw, and adorned his garden on Cabanne Avenue for many years, then were given to the Missouri Botanical Garden.

F. JOHANSON KREBS

Close-up of one stone lantern now in the Missouri Botanical Garden.

Olympics

MAN'S most primitive type of transportation—his own two feet—also had a world-renowned showing here in the Olympic Games of 1904.

The ancient Olympic Games of Greece have intrigued man from time immemorial, and a revival was someday sure to follow the Roman decree of 396 A.D., forbidding these contests. Exactly fifteen centuries later in 1896 the games were restored in Athens, with awards distributed by the King. The 1900 Olympics were next held in Paris, and Chicago was then scheduled for the 1904 Games. However, the International Olympic Committee, realizing that there would be a devastating effect on attendance if a Chicago celebration was planned when a Universal Exposition was occurring in St. Louis, decided to grant the privilege to St. Louis.

Since a well-organized Physical Culture Exhibition was planned for the Fair—with excellent buildings and equipment for the first time at any fair—it seemed reasonable to incorporate the Olympic Games into this program. At the request of the President of the Olympic Committee it was designated that all athletic events held during the Exposition bear the name "Olympic Events," even though the specific Olympic contests themselves occurred only during the week of August 29 to September 4.

Washington University's new and modern gymnasium and athletic field were the scenes of those games, while swimming events took place in the United States Life Saving Exhibition Lake, formerly a pond at what is now Wydown and Skinker. Francis Gymnasium and Francis Field are still in use today, and by their names honor Exposition President David R. Francis.

Plaque on Francis Field gatepost.

Only a few nations—England, Germany, France, Ireland, Scotland and Australia— sent competitors, and the United States won most of the events, capturing twenty-one of the twenty-two track and field events. The one attracting the most attention was the Marathon. Thirty-one runners ran over a twenty-four-mile course through St. Louis County. Even though it was an excessively warm day, just one water stop was allowed. Only fourteen finished the race, Thomas Hicks of the United States being the winner. This first Olympiad ever to be held on United States soil lent much prestige to the Fair.

Les Femmes

 THE Feminist Movement, so prominent a part of the present scene, actually had its origins one hundred fifty years ago. Activity had become quite brisk by 1872 even though it would be another half century before woman suffrage would be granted (1922). The planners of the 1904 Fair were sensitive to this movement and the temper of the administration seemed amazingly moderate toward it. Women were considered "leaders of thought and action," and their accomplishments were to be recognized equally with men. To that end a Board of Lady Managers was established with the selection of twenty-three prominent women representing every section of the nation.

So intent were these ladies on the idea of equality that there was to be no separate woman's building which might serve to designate any apartness; accordingly they were granted some meeting rooms in one of the Washington University buildings.

However fractious their organization, with many inner dissensions—as reported frequently by the news accounts—it must be admitted that this Board achieved many of its goals and made an important contribution to the rights of women at that time. One of the resolutions which they adopted was "that there be no indecent dances in the midways or improper exhibits at the Exposition." Whether or not this expressed position had an influence on the high morals of the Pike—indeed of the whole Fair —cannot be ascertained.

Ladies' Protagonist

UNDOUBTEDLY the advance of the Feminist Movement in that day was directly related to the two magazines enjoying the widest circulation of the time—*The Woman's Magazine* and *The Woman's Farm Journal* (circulation 1,500,000). Both of these magazines were published in what is now University City by Edward Gardner Lewis, a far-sighted man with keen business acumen and also some grandiose plans, most of which never came to fruition. He was a strong proponent of Women's Rights and his two magazines were definitely effective in helping women to establish themselves.

Through the nation-wide coverage of the news of the Fair in his magazines the Exposition received such broad publicity that great numbers of visitors were drawn from across the nation and even from foreign countries.

Lewis built the handsome, octagonal Magazine Building with its ornate interiors and marble staircases (now the City Hall of University City) as well

as other nearby buildings associated with the publishing of these magazines. During the Fair a huge searchlight, the largest in the world, on top of the Magazine Building, swept a wide beam of light nightly over the Fair Grounds. The light was originally designed as a part of Russia's exhibit, but when those plans had to be abandoned because of internal problems, Lewis secured it for his building and astonished visitors with its broad mysterious beam. After being forgotten

City Hall of University City, formerly Lewis' Magazine Building. Note giant searchlight, used for the first time on Opening Night of Fair. Everyone was amazed as its placement had been kept a secret.

for many years, this great light and its mechanism were reconditioned in 1967 and it is once again in service with a powerful beam that shines with far-reaching brilliance at appropriate, important civic events.

North and west of the Magazine Building Lewis set up a vast tent city (Camp Lewis) which provided inexpensive lodging and simple meals for thousands. Though Lewis had some strange traits that worked to his disadvantage, his contributions to the success of the Fair have never been adequately recognized and should be properly acknowledged.

Women, Artistic and Otherwise

ALTHOUGH many today might be tempted to think that the Feminist Movement at this Fair was merely rhetorical, nevertheless the contributions of women were quite prominently visible everywhere. Prior to the opening of the Fair ten women sculptors were at work and each one's creation won a place of distinction. Most prominent among these was the "Victory" statue adorning the dome of Festival Hall, which brought lasting fame to the designer not only due to its excellence but also because for the first time "Victory" was depicted as a man instead of the legendary woman. Trophy manufacturers immediately appropriated this design and for many years it was the figure seen on athletic awards. The statue on the dome of the Missouri Building—"The Spirit of Missouri"—was also designed by a woman, as was the entire interior sculpture work of the United States Government Building. Women were represented by their paintings in the Art Palace, and several prominent women organists were invited to give concerts on the organ in Festival Hall.

Other women made the news. One, just emerging, would become a world figure, Helen Keller. The blind and deaf senior at Radcliffe College, and her equally famous teacher, Annie Sullivan, were invited to spend a week at the Fair officially representing all the deaf and blind. And again, a little-known New York City woman doctor created a mild crisis when she appeared in the ladies' lounge in a "pants suit" and was denied entrance. A strong supporter of the Feminist Movement, she eventually produced adequate identification and was received, but not without some titillating news reports in the local papers.

A new kind of liberation was granted many women visitors in the attractive nursery located in the Model City, maintained in the most modern manner so that parents could enjoy the wonders of the Fair unencumbered by their young off-spring.

Although not originally intended for Festival Hall, "Victory," by Evelyn B. Longman, so enchanted the Fair designers that it won this position of distinction.

Copy of the summer palace of Prince Pu Lun.

Chinese Prince

EVERY Fair has its celebrity visitors and most prominent of these at the 1904 Fair was the Chinese Prince Pu Lun. China for the first time in history was officially participating in a universal exposition and after such a long seclusion this debut was quite an important one, with a three-pronged thrust: (1) the exquisite Chinese Pavilion on the Washington University campus; (2) a vast collection of Chinese products displayed in the Liberal Arts Building; and (3) a Chinese village on the Pike which introduced visitors to a taste of Chinese culture.

The Chinese Pavilion was an artistic reproduction of Prince Pu Lun's summer palace at Peking. All the materials were brought here from China and the palace constructed by native Chinese artisans.

The exhibit in the Liberal Arts Palace expressed China's desire to show her face to the world. An extensive array of hand-wrought and machine-wrought articles—bronzes, porcelains, silks, carved wood, four thousand fans of various styles and a collection of one hundred different models of boats used in China—were a part of the display. Many of these articles were purchased by St. Louisans at the close of the Fair, and thus in many homes and shops today some of these prized wares may be seen.

The Chinese Village on the Pike, brought to the Fair by Chinese merchants of Philadelphia, introduced the curious to Chinese culture. A theatre with native performers, a joss house, a tea-house and a bazaar were features to captivate the sight-seers.

Prince Pu Lun arrived at the Fair for the opening ceremony and was much impressed with the grandeur of the scene. Grandson of the late Emperor, the 29 year old Prince stayed in St. Louis for two months, living at the George Washington Hotel on Kingshighway and Washington. Honored at many festive affairs, he returned the honors with several brilliant functions of his own. His charming personality and simplicity of manner endeared him to all.

Likewise, he was charmed with President Francis, and in gratitude for his friendship, he bequeathed the entire Chinese Pavilion to him personally. At this time, Mr. Francis lived in his own mansion on Newstead and Maryland, and concern was expressed as to what disposition should be made of this munificent gift. Some thought that Mr. Francis should have it moved to Forest Park for the enjoyment of the people of St. Louis. Others felt that it should be moved to another part of the University's campus and used as a foreign language center. Unfortunately the final disposition of it is clouded,

although some of its wood carvings and ivory inlays have been used in the decor of at least one St. Louis home.

Other distinguished visitors from foreign states were: Cardinal Satolli, special representative of the Pope; Prince Hohenlohe-Schillingfuerst of Germany; Prince Henry of Prussia; the Crown Prince of Siam; Prince Fushimi of Japan; Vice-president Ramon Corral of Mexico; and Baron von Sternberg, the German Ambassador.

One of the hundreds of ivory-inlaid panels from the Chinese Pavilion now all privately owned.

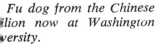

Fu dog from the Chinese ilion now at Washington versity.

Art - Symbolism - Allegory

THE beauty of buildings such as the Chinese Pavilion could not be noted without also observing the artistic touches so evident over the whole of the Fair Grounds.

When Director of Works Isaac Taylor, a St. Louis architect, contemplated the layout of the Fair Grounds, he wanted a feeling of openness with broad vistas, not buildings thrust against buildings as in other Fairs. Thus, nothing was quite so propitious as the selection of Forest Park for the site. The lower plain, the higher levels of forest area, and the broad connecting slopes formed a topography most alluring to his dreams. *And so he envisioned an open fan.* The contour of Art Hill was ideal for this plan and he laid out the Grounds with all the buildings, avenues and plazas radiating from a point just behind the present Art Museum—the spot where the first stake had been driven.

To perfect this radial plan, the palaces surrounding the Grand Basin were assigned certain sizes and shapes, though much freedom was allowed the architects in the further design of the buildings. Director Taylor desired to achieve a sense of symbolism in this overall design, which was further developed by the appropriate names assigned to the plazas, avenues and bridges, and also by the use of sculpture which was under the direction of Karl Bitter.

"The Protest of the Sioux."

Statue of Meriwether Lewis, famous explorer, who with William Clark left St. Louis in May, 1804, to explore the Louisiana Purchase Territory and make their way to the Pacific Coast.

The staggering amount of sculptured pieces—twelve hundred statues in addition to ornate sculptured decorations on the palaces—was so masterfully arranged by Mr. Bitter that the effect perfectly complemented Mr. Taylor's envisioned design. The principal work of sculpture, Mr. Bitter's own Louisiana Purchase Monument, was constructed with a speaker's platform on one side, and the high-relief of the Signing of the Louisiana Purchase Treaty on the opposite side. This high-relief now occupies a place in the loggia of the Jefferson Memorial Building.

Mr. Bitter, whose talents were represented in other figures on the Grounds, called upon almost one-hundred other sculptors whose works amplified the design of the layout. His excellent arrangement of historical statues led the viewer to see first the early explorers, then Indian chiefs, followed by the Indians' pathetic destiny, then the men of government and foreign affairs, and Napoleon and Jefferson—all so significantly placed as to lead the stroller down the avenue of history. At entrances of each palace stood statues of men particularly related to that certain field of endeavor. Much of this sculpture was of temporary material, but several permanent pieces were given to the city; others were destined to be displayed permanently in the future St. Louis Art Museum.

Nature's Art

HE artistic landscaping, carried out under the direction of George E. Kessler, noted landscape architect, also complemented the work of Mr. Taylor. In the short time allotted for horticultural development, over five-hundred trees, large and small, were planted and vigilantly nurtured to adequate growth so that shade would enrich the broad lawns. Beautiful formal gardens provided a continuous display of nature's flamboyant colors and Mr. Kessler's floral work reached the pinnacle of success in the formal gardens beside each cascade on Art Hill.

The crystal-clear splashing water of the cascades was only possible because of the foresight of President Francis and Mayor Wells. Until this time St. Louis' water supply, though safe, was disgracefully muddy. Many residents relied on bottled water for home use. Knowing that muddy water would mar the beauty of the grand scene, the officials arranged to call in experts to renovate the city's water supply. The Chain-of-Rocks settling basins and water purification system developed at that time resulted in an excellent city water system that has enjoyed a national reputation for the past seventy years, and the stunning effect of the cascades was saved.

Walk along the Grand Basin.

One of the many bandstands, all alike, which dotted the Fair Grounds.

Music

THE song, "Meet Me in St. Louis, Louis" (sung as, "St. Louie, Louie"), born on the Pike, has joined the immortals of American folk music, but the Pike was not the only source of music. American feet tapped to many types, although band music was undoubtedly the most popular variety during this period of our nation's history. Every city and town had its own home-grown band and the nation was dotted with plain and fancy bandstands. On the Fair Grounds many unpretentious bandstands were located at strategic spots, but the largest one could accommodate three bands at once and must have been very showy at a cost of $8000!

Characteristic of a fair is the sound of many kinds of music and the St. Louis Fair was no exception. An appropriation of $450,000 granted for the total program was under the directorship of the well-known St. Louis musician Ernest R. Kroeger. News accounts of the time carry stories of concerts, music conventions, guest organists, choirs, orchestras, bands and solo artists in a continual flow for the seven months of the Fair. Besides the well-loved John Phillip Sousa and his band who were here for several engagements, many other noted ones performed in the various bandstands on the Grounds. Government military bands gave concerts daily at the United States Government Building and almost every foreign village gave forth native music, some with primitive instruments. The Exposition's own official band was under the direction of St. Louisan William Weil.

The St. Louis Choral Symphony under the direction of Mr. Alfred Ernst rendered some of the more serious music and the long list of guest symphony conductors included the name of the well-known Walter Damrosch. To lure Fair-goers to the "heavier" brand of music, *The Official Guide to the World's Fair* promised that "the programs would be dignified without being too severe"—and all for an admission fee of only 25c!

Interesting Trivia

TINTYPES and daguerreotypes were already a thing of the past, having been replaced by photography, by now a well-established industry. Although there were numerous American photographers at work daily behind their black hoods—including an official lady photographer!—most of the excellent photographic displays in the exhibition palaces were not submitted by Americans but were from foreign nations. Commercial photography at the Fair was closely guarded and rather stringent controls were in effect. However, some 36,000 photographs were made, preserved and can be seen today in a number of picture albums, each one claiming to be the "official photographs of the Fair." In the early 1950's a technique was perfected whereby many of these pictures could be combined in a series to result in a "moving picture." Consequently, even though movies had not yet emerged in 1904, an amazingly realistic motion picture of the Fair was made. This was greatly enjoyed by thousands when viewed as a television documentary sponsored by a local utility, its popularity resulting in a number of showings in the 1960's and 70's.

During the Fair the United States Government minted 200,000 gold dollars, called the "World's Fair Gold Dollar." Some of these coins show up occasionally, and logically, more are seen in the St. Louis

Official Lady Photographer. All photographers were carefully screened and closely supervised. Pictures of certain sizes only were permitted, and other such similar strict regulations were in effect.

F. Johansen-Krebs

area than elsewhere. In 1973 each coin was valued at $140 to $150. Likewise, the United States Postal Service issued five commemorative stamps honoring the Louisiana Purchase. The value of this set in mint condition is $139.50.

Some of the products exhibited in 1904 may surprise the sophisticates of the 1970's. One, the DeForest Wireless Telegraph Tower was the forerunner of modern radio transmission equipment. Signor Marconi of Italy, whose invention made wireless messages possible, was a distinguished visitor to the Fair and, of course, to the Wireless Tower. Messages were sent daily from the Tower to the downtown newspaper offices, and before the end of the Fair, news items were being flashed all the way to Chicago. . . . On the Pike one could view a *statisticum*—a Swedish invention which mechanized statistics—perhaps an embryonic computer? . . . Coin-changers were in use and liquid air was being demonstrated. . . . X-rays were making their debut, as were electric clocks, automatic telephones and a telephone answering device. . . . A "photoscope" advertisement in a magazine claimed it to be the only self-operating picture-taking machine in the world; there were two-hundred of them on the Grounds and the ad suggests "Take six nickels and make six photos every minute."

People on the concourse to DeForest Wireless Telegraph Tower — Electricity Day, September 13, 1904.

Fresh in the memory of every Fair visitor was the Boer War. Lest its glories die unsung, it was re-enacted each day in a semi-circular area on the Skinker hillside. Bleacher seats provided comfortable viewing while real fire-arms blasted away. (No deaths reported and no British soldiers downed.)

In the Liberal Arts Palace a twenty-five foot high soap bubble fountain delighted the children as they watched 176,000 bubbles per minute floating lazily down. Adults must have been surprised to learn that only three-quarters of a pound of soap would produce those bubbles continuously for two days.

The Gulch, an area near the Plateau of States, was the scene of all types of mining processes, including a coal mine, a placer mine, oil-drilling rigs, and the only exhibit of the cyanide process ever shown at a fair. And for amazing amusement, each day Borax Bill drove his twenty-mule team through the streets of the Plateau of States demonstrating this Death Valley operation to fascinated onlookers.

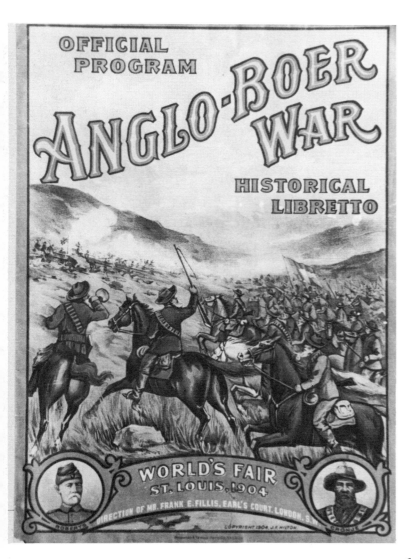

Conventions and congresses meeting almost continuously during the seven months had their head-quarters in the Hall of Congresses (Ridgley Library) on the Washington University campus. The most notable among the one hundred eighty-six which convened at the Fair was the National Democratic Convention of 1904, which nominated Alton B. Parker.

And, A. S. Aloe had a concession to sell smoked glasses!

A program of the Boer War, fought daily at the Fair. The scenes on the battlefield were realistic in detail and the roar of battle reached such strength as to be heard throughout the Exposition Grounds.

Hall of Congresses, present Ridgley Hall (Washington University Campus).

Detail of ceiling in former auditorium at the Fair, now Holmes Student Center in Ridgley Hall.

Gates to Westmoreland Place. In this private place was one of the greatest concentrations of wealth in the United States from the 1890's to the 1920's.

Perimeter

JUST outside the boundaries of the Fair Grounds, the western part of St. Louis was developing rapidly with many beautiful residential areas. The "private places" so characteristic of St. Louis were already displaying many handsome and costly new mansions, and nearby high-rise apartment buildings added to the atmosphere of elegance. According to President Francis, more people in St. Louis owned their own homes than in any city of its size in this country or in Europe. At this time, too, St. Luke's Hospital opened its new building on Delmar.

And an even larger structure on DeBaliviere haunts the memory of many St. Louisans. Known later on as the "Winter Garden," it was originally built to house the "jai alai" court and grandstand. "Jai alai" was a popular game of Spanish origin somewhat similar to handball but played with special equipment on an exceptionally long court. Tournaments were held during the Fair, but afterwards interest declined and the building became, for several years, St. Louis' only ice-skating rink. Not a few are nostalgic about the Saturdays spent there as children learning to skate and then mastering intricate figures on the ice. In the 1960's the building was razed in favor of a super-market.

West of the city limits, an imposing hotel known as The Epworth Hotel during the Fair may be seen today—the Christian Old People's Home in University City.

...e of Robert S. Brookings on Lindell Boule-
...where many of the world's important people
...entertained during the Fair. Brookings, pres-
...of Washington University's Board of Trus-
...arranged to have present Brookings Hall
...pleted in time to be used as the Fair's Admin-
...tion Building.

*Christian Old People's Home, formerly
The Epworth Hotel, located at 6600
Washington Avenue, University City.*

67

Fires

THE almost-total wooden construction of the main buildings and the massive uncovered wooden trusses supporting the roofs of each structure were open invitations to disastrous fires, and the Fair was not immune. Many small fires were easily handled by concession operators or the Fair's official fire fighters. There were only four major fires, one of which occurred after closing day. When several persons remarked to Mr. Francis, "How lucky!" his response claimed that luck played no part at all, that the watchfulness and alertness of the vigilant force of fire inspectors were responsible for the good record and the fact that there was no loss of life. Today several ludicrous-looking fire plugs can be seen dotting the wide-open golf links—relics of the excellent fire-fighting equipment installed for the Fair and never removed.

One of the four fires resulted in the destruction of the Missouri Building, two were in concessions (Ancient Rome and Jerusalem) and the other was the House of Hoo-Hoo.

Curiosity over this comical name led to the information that the Concatenated Order of Hoo-Hoo is an organization of lumbermen who banded together in 1892, the order having continued without interruption to this day. Headquartered in Boston, the order has active groups across the nation and sponsors a national convention. The name "Hoo-Hoo" has nothing to do with the call of lumbermen at work in the forests as some might suppose, but happens to be a whimsical name adopted in a moment of frivolity at the time of its organization.

The House of Hoo-Hoo was designed to display representative finished woods native to the United States. Each of the rooms on the first floor was finished in a different wood and the main auditorium, seating 350, was done in yellow pine. Members of the fraternal order, their families and friends were particularly urged to visit the house, but the exhibition was, of course, open to the public. The building, totally destroyed by fire on June 24th, was completely rebuilt within thirty days—an example of extraordinary energy and enterprise. The hope that the city of St. Louis would use the building and convert it into a permanent exhibition of the lumbering industry failed; in the end it had to face demolition.

The House of Hoo-Hoo.

A Sad Farewell

THROUGH all the crisp, beautiful days of the 1904 autumn, still they came—crowds surging through the gates and holding fast to this gem so soon to escape their clasp. For the Fair had become a prized possession of all St. Louisans. Each one felt a personal attachment to it because of its sheer grandeur; because of the new stimulus given to the city; and because it had been their own successful affair. And so as December approached there was a sadness everywhere.

The Exposition closed at midnight on December 1, 1904. The day had been decreed "Francis Day" to honor the president of this greatest of world's fairs. From early morn until midnight thousands of St. Louisans gathered to pay him homage, for it had been declared by the Governor of Missouri that this was to be as total a holiday as possible—schools were closed and every business that was able suspended operations. It was the merriest, yet the saddest day of the year. It was like a carnival, yet like a funeral. But all joined in to make a continuous succession of personal ovations to Mr. Francis equalled only by those accorded the President of the United States when he had made his official visit.

President Francis was escorted by officials from his home via private trolley car to the entrance gates where an escort of the Jefferson Guards received him, then accompanied him for a last visit to his office in the Administration Building. Activities and speeches continued throughout the day, and finally, in the late afternoon, a reception was held, followed by a last trip over the Fair Grounds and then a banquet in the great ball below the Tyrolean Alps.

Before midnight, President Francis and his party drove the length of the Pike. The crowds pressed against his coach and spirits ran high. The cheering and demonstrations as the coach crept over the mile-long avenue were of unbounded friendliness and admiration.

It was one of the wildest nights ever witnessed in St. Louis, but careful vigilance and orderly authority intercepted any possibility of an unpleasant spectacle. Finally, the party proceeded to the Plaza of St. Louis where, at the Louisiana Purchase Monument which was strung with colored lights, President Francis appeared and was given a mighty ovation. When he spoke, he said, "I am about to perform a heart-rending duty." His hand swept over the scene of palaces glimmering with their thousands of electric lights and he "wished they might live forever." As the midnight hour approached, he expressed appreciation to all who had helped make the Fair a success, then raising both arms toward the great buildings, he said:

"Farewell, a long farewell to all thy splendor." Total darkness covered the Grounds as he threw the switch. The band played "Auld Lang Syne." Then suddenly the air was brilliant with the light of fireworks. "Farewell" was spelled out in bright colors on one wall, "Good Night" on another, then the features of President Francis were seen in blazing outline.

It was the end of the Universal Exposition of 1904.

"Farewell, a long farewell to all thy splendor."
—David R. Francis, December 1, 1904.

Demolition

HE loss by fire of the Missouri Building on November 19th was almost like a prelude to the devastation soon to come to the whole Fair, for on December 2, 1904, it was scheduled for demolition. Destruction was begun by the Chicago Housewrecking Company, the firm which had purchased the contract for $450,000, and demolition was to be completed within six months. Even though the Fair was officially closed, visitors were allowed in the Grounds at half price (25c) to watch the passing of the scene. When ticket-takers could no longer be hired, entrance was free.

The demolition process produced crushed "staff"—mountains of it! Useful only for landfill, it was hauled away over several miles of railroad tracks which had been laid down prior to the Fair for bringing in the construction materials. These tracks, cleverly covered over with asphalt, had been hidden during the Fair. By pealing off the asphalt they were re-exposed at the time of demolition, thus providing a quick method for transporting the debris from the Grounds.

Grant's Cabin, originally located on South Rock Hill Road, went through a series of moves before being brought to the Fair Grounds where it was used by the Blanke Coffee Company. Unwanted at the close of the Fair, it was finally purchased by Adolphus Busch, an admirer of Grant, and moved to its present site on Gravois Road.

The exhibition buildings were removed in record time, others moved out at a slower pace. But the Pike became the city's worst problem as the concessions could hardly be given away, much less sold. Consequently some of them stood for many months and the city planners, eager to get on with the restoration process, became quite agitated.

The States' buildings were the easiest to dispose of. Many, made of permanent materials, were of a size serviceable to a family, thus several were purchased and hauled to nearby sites for summer or permanent homes. The New Jersey House was moved to Kirkwood and until recently (1972) served as an apartment building. It is now demolished. The New Hampshire House, quite altered from the original, may be seen today on Litzinger Road.

Oklahoma was scheduled to be transported to El Reno, Oklahoma, to serve as a club building for the Elks' Lodge.

Michigan and Minnesota were slated for permanent fair buildings in their home states.

Belgium's windowless palace, purchased by Anheuser-Busch and used for many years for their glass works.

New Mexico would become a public library building in Santa Fe.

Iowa was transported to that state to become an asylum for alcoholics.

The Temple of Fraternity, rated the most sanitary building at the Fair, was shipped to New Mexico and re-erected as the largest sanitarium in the world for consumptives.

The Swedish Building was moved to Lindsborg, Kansas, to house the Art Department of Bethany College.

Brazil's white palace was rebuilt in Rio de Janeiro.

Belgium's massive, windowless structure, purchased by Anheuser-Busch, Incorporated, was moved to the brewery site in South St. Louis where it served through the years as the firm's glass works, although now no longer in existence.

The Wireless Tower was removed to Creve Coeur Lake in the county.

The 50-foot statue of Vulcan, donation of the city of Birmingham, Alabama, was returned (on seven freight cars) and lay a-rusting for many years, and only recently, was restored atop a hill overlooking the city.

The renowned Blarney Castle in the Irish Village was a theatre in which a company of Dublin players entertained in the true Celtic spirit.

The statue known as the "Fountain Angel", by Romanelli, located at the Lindell-Skinker entrance to Forest Park at the time of the Fair, was later moved to the interior of the park where unfortunately it has been badly vandalized. When restored it will be placed in the vicinity of the Municipal Opera as a relic of the Fair.

Other pieces of statuary were given to the city and assigned to various parks and public places but their whereabouts have been lost through the years.

An attempt was made to make the whole Pike a permanent fixture—a sort of St. Louis "Coney Island." The Tyrolean Alps, an especially attractive concession, was the stimulus to this plan. However, Washington University officials viewed such an amusement center as an unhealthy distraction to the nearby academic campus. Then Adolphus Busch purchased the Alps, planning to install them as an attraction in Forest Park, linking it with a summer theatre. This plan, too, did not materialize and they were eventually destroyed!

Fair Japan, a concession on the Pike, contained a copy of an old temple which many St. Louisans may remember as the oriental entertainment pavilion at the Forest Park Highlands Amusement Park on Oakland Avenue, where it was installed when the Fair was over.

Some of the buildings which had cost thousands of dollars to construct were sold for less than one hundred dollars. Quite a few buildings and statues were lent to the Lewis and Clark Exposition which was held in Portland, Oregon, in 1905. Final disposition of these "lends" is obscure.

"The Fountain Angel"
presented as a gift to the city.

After the demolition of the Fair, restoration of Forest Park was placed under the direction of Mr. Kessler, landscape architect, his plan being to make the park even more beautiful than it had been before. There was no attempt to restore it to its former condition as some of the trees had been cut down to make way for the palaces. Modern ecologists, however, would be glad to note that even then wanton destruction of vegetation was not to be tolerated and only a few necessary removals had been made.

"The Wilderness" could not be restored and the cascades on Art Hill had to be removed. Lakes and lagoons were modified, and large meadows and lawns (including the present golf course) were developed and beautified. The area behind the Art Museum was planted with 75,000 trees and shrubs for later transplanting to other parts of the park. Most of the six and one-half miles of Exposition roads were kept with a permanent paving added, and some of the bridges were retained. Skinker Road, merely a wide pathway before the Fair, was graded and beautified.

After three years of labor, the restoration was finally complete and, even in those pre-inflationary days, the cost was estimated at one million dollars.

One of the fire plugs left on the golf course in Forest Park.

The St. Louis Art Museum at night.

What is Left?

A FEW specific gifts were bequeathed to the city following the close of the Fair which are impressive mementoes of St. Louis' notable Exposition. Prominent among these are the donations of the Exposition Company itself:

The Art Museum
The two statues flanking the entrance to the Museum
The statue of St. Louis in front of the Museum
The World's Fair Pavilion (constructed 1908-09)

The Bird Cage was left to the City by the Smithsonian Institution and the Jefferson Memorial Building was a three-way gift.

By agreement before the construction of the Exposition buildings, it had been planned that the permanent Art Palace would be given to the city for a public Art Museum. Until this time, the Museum of Fine Arts, located at Nineteenth and Locust Street, had served in this capacity, having originated in 1874 as an outgrowth of free evening drawing classes sponsored by Washington University. St. Louis thus gained a handsome new million-dollar museum, with many fine pieces of statuary and paintings left from the Fair.

It was first occupied in 1906 by the Museum of Fine Arts, which was then still a department of Washington University. Records show that the first exhibit in this building was held in September, 1906. In 1907 it was firmly established as "The City Art Museum of St. Louis" by the people of St. Louis, who voted to tax themselves for its maintenance. (At this time Washington University relinquished its connection and established other quarters.)

The action by St. Louisans to support their museum in this manner makes the museum a singular institution, as there is no record of any other community thus taxing itself. The action of this law was delayed until its constitutionality was affirmed by the Supreme Court of Missouri in 1911, but during the intervening years the museum was open to thousands of visitors. Since 1911 the tax (2c on $100 valuation) has been continuously effective. Some private funds have supplemented this sustaining foundation, and in 1971, the establishment of the Zoo-Museum District has made additional monies available for financial support.

"Sculpture"

Daniel Chester French

Two statues at the entrance of the Art Palace, "Painting" and "Sculpture" were originally made of "staff," and the Exposition Company requested the two sculptors, Louis Saint-Gaudens and Daniel Chester French to refashion their original figures in marble (at a cost of $10,000) for a permanent embellishment to the handsome St. Louis Art Museum.

"Painting"

Louis Saint-Gaudens

The Statue of St. Louis by Charles Niehaus, located during the Fair at the head of the Plaza of St. Louis, was the first large piece of statuary to greet the visitor passing through the main entrance gates. Titled "The Apotheosis of St. Louis" it had a massive base on which was a figure representing the city of St. Louis extending her hand in a gracious welcome to her guests. Since the statue was not made of permanent materials, the Exposition Company had it recast in bronze, at a cost of $40,000, removed the welcoming figure, and then relocated it on its present site at the top of Art Hill. On October 4, 1906, it was unveiled, and, with the Art Museum, given to the citizens of St. Louis.

The thirteenth-century King Louis IX of France for whom this city is named, elevated to sainthood twenty-seven years after his death because of his piety, justice and kindness, was the patron saint of Louis XV, monarch of Pierre Laclede, founder of this city. Hence the name of the city—St. Louis. It is interesting to note that "Louisiana Territory," so named by the explorer LaSalle, honors King Louis XIV of France.

"The Apotheosis of St. Louis was intended to express the welcome which the city of St. Louis extended to her guests, and to commemorate the character in history for whom the World's Fair city was named, Louis IX of France known as 'St. Louis.'"
—David R. Francis Unveiling ceremonies, October 4, 1906.

Jefferson Memorial viewed from the south. A large new underground addition has recently been completed.

A Commendable Memorial

IT IS fitting that one of the finest legacies of the Fair to the city of St. Louis should be the Jefferson Memorial, standing symbolically at the former main entrance to the Fair Grounds. Isaac S. Taylor, Chairman of the Commission of Architects for the Exposition, was the designer.

The idea of a monument to Thomas Jefferson, third president of the United States, was not a new one. In the 1880's James G. Blaine declaimed that it was a reproach that nowhere in the Louisiana Purchase Territory was there any monument to this great man—indeed there was none *anywhere* in the whole of the United States. The only monument that might have been considered to honor him was an obelisk which, in 1885, was erected to supplant his own self-designed shaft marking his last resting place at Monticello. When his unpretentious shaft was replaced by the more fitting obelisk, Missouri University at Columbia acquired the Jefferson-designed shaft, where it remains on view to this day. It bears this epitaph, written by him:

"Here was buried Thomas Jefferson, author of the Declaration of Independence, of the statute of Virginia for religious freedom, and father of the University of Virginia."

Statue of Thomas Jefferson by Karl Bitter, in loggia of Jefferson Memorial Building, dedicated April 30, 1913. Bitter arranged to have a block of marble weighing forty-five tons shipped to the site and placed on the pedestal where he then carved the massive statue. This was done to prevent damage in shipment.

From the earliest days of the Fair's planning, a sentiment was expressed that some enduring, large monument should result from it.

Thus, in 1909, President Francis, in settlement of loans and funds, requested the United States Government to participate with the city of St. Louis and the Exposition Company in constructing a memorial to Thomas Jefferson. The proposition was well received, Congress stipulating that the Exposition Company should erect a monument to cost not less than $200,000.

The cornerstone was laid on May 1, 1911, and the building completed in 1913. Of Bedford stone, it has a center loggia in which the massive seated figure of Thomas Jefferson, sculptured by Karl Bitter, commands attention. The loggia is flanked on each side by a large wing, each one serving as a repository for historical documents significant of the Louisiana Purchase Territory. The Missouri Historical Society and a library maintained by the Society are also housed here.

*"The instrument we have signed will c«
no tears to flow. It will prepare centurie
happiness for innumerable generations
the human race."*
—Robert Livingston
Upon the signing of the Louis:
Purchase Treaty.

Also in the loggia Karl Bitter's famous high-relief of the signing of the
Louisiana Purchase Treaty may be seen. This work which was a part of the
Louisiana Purchase Monument during the Fair, depicts Monroe, Marbois
and Livingston putting their signatures on the historical document of acqui-
sition. The treaty was dated April 30, 1803, but actually signed several days
later.

The Jefferson Memorial was a commitment of the City, the Federal Government and the Exposition Company. Thus it stands as a monument not only to the president who helped make the whole of the West a possibility, but
also to the spirit of the citizens of St. Louis, the trust and cooperation of the
United States Government, and the dedication of the men of vision who guid-
ed the St. Louis World's Fair to its grand culmination.

A ticket for one of the special events held continuously throughout the Fair.

Fair balloons. Note top of thirty-foot fence which enclosed balloon area (on present Washington University campus).

Advertisement for the famous Inside Inn, founded by E. M. Statler, from which came the inspiration for his chain of hotels. There was an Outside Inn located at Delmar and Hamilton.

But the Fair lives on—in the memories of those yet alive who fell under its spell; in the gracious gifts bestowed upon the city; in the thousands of pictures and documents in libraries and museums; and in countless souvenirs and mementoes cherished by their owners. Handsome Chinese hand-carved tables and chairs, silver souvenir spoons, inlaid panels and carvings, even gaudy badges, ribbons, pendants and "The World's Fair in a Nutshell"—from the souvenir stands—are proudly displayed in both unpretentious and elegant homes throughout the city, as the value of such mementoes and interest in the Fair continues to rise in an ever-increasing force. For the less fortunate, displays of Fair memorabilia may be viewed in the Jefferson Memorial.

The city of St. Louis has experienced only one international exposition in its history and citizens proudly claim it to have been the most glorious of all fairs, as well as the only one (until very recent years) to have realized a financial profit. However prejudiced these claims may be, this Fair has been hailed as surpassing all others in beauty, embellishment and variety. The fact remains that geographically it was the largest of all times. St. Louisans can be proud that their Fair has attained a position of distinction among all fairs, and has indelibly imprinted its success upon the city's future.

License tag used for official automobiles at the Fair.

The World's Fair in a Nutshell

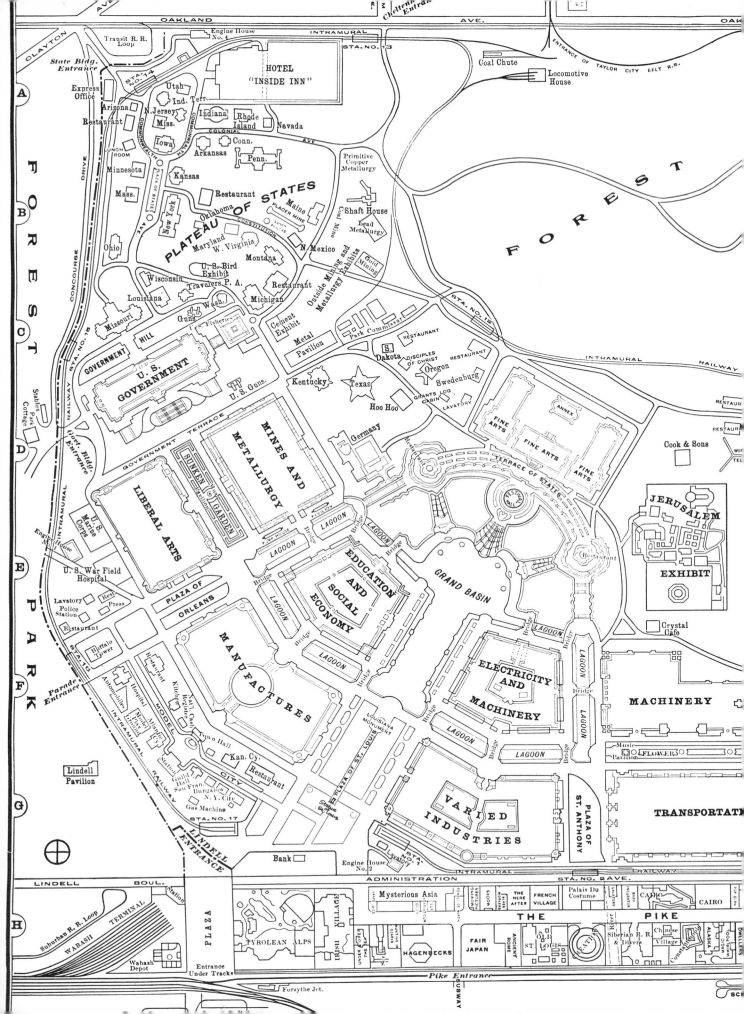

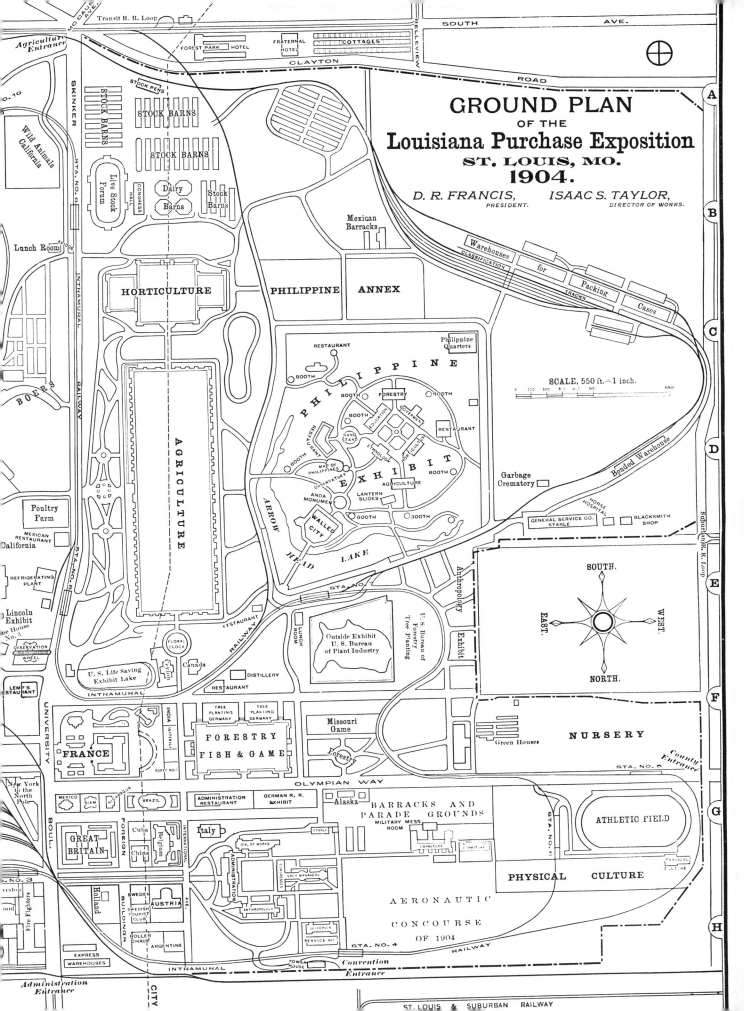

GROUND PLAN
OF THE
Louisiana Purchase Exposition
ST. LOUIS, MO.
1904.

D. R. FRANCIS,
PRESIDENT.

ISAAC S. TAYLOR,
DIRECTOR OF WORKS.

SCALE, 550 ft.=1 inch.

Appendix

WHY fairs? What is their origin? Their meaning? Their purpose?

Undoubtedly fairs originated from a very simple act—a shrewd merchant took his articles to a neighboring village and discovered that business picked up. And possibly to his surprise, he found some worthy merchandise to carry home with him.

The earliest recorded fairs were in Asia and Africa and are mentioned in the Bible, for instance—"Tarshish . . . they traded in thy fairs"—Ezek. 27:12. "Tyre . . . she is a mart of all nations"—Isaiah 23:3. Because crowds were attracted, trade became more active and vice-versa—one fed upon the other. Coastal fairs brought glamour articles from across the seas.

The earliest fair as a "market" is recorded as having occurred in Britain in 208 A.D. France had one in 427 A.D.—but more as a political gathering than for trade. Fairs also became associated with religion when the faithful began making pilgrimages and the Crusades became popular. Sometimes they were associated with the Church and then were called "festivals." It is not surprising to read that the great cholera epidemics coincided with the great fairs.

Eventually commerce became so important a part of fairs that they were put under royal supervision, and by the Middle Ages they were held under charters granted by kings. People would travel as much as one hundred miles to attend. Week-long fairs allowed time for merry-making for those living lonely lives on farms. There were an estimated thirty-three hundred fairs in the thirteenth century.

To France is accorded the honor of originating the "Exposition." In a 1798 fair, Napoleon awarded gold medals for achievements and thus he is credited with the idea of the exposition. France went giddy over this "invention" as records indicate she subsequently held expositions in 1801, 06, 19, 23, 27, 30, 39, 44, and 49.

The idea of a World's Fair was first conceived by Prince Albert of England, and in 1851 the "Great Exhibition of the Works of All Nations" opened in the Crystal Palace—an immense building made entirely of glass over a light metal framework. It was like a giant sparkling greenhouse. Forty nations exhibited and it was so successful that New York followed in 1853 with her own Crystal Palace. Munich had one in 1854 but an outbreak of cholera marred its success. Paris wouldn't be outdone—her first international exposition was in 1855. Then followed a stream of expositions, each one exceeding the others in size and splendor.

In the United States, the Centennial Exposition in Philadelphia in 1876 commemorated United States Independence, but unfortunately, insufficient time was allowed for planning and construction so that on opening day many of the buildings had not yet been completed. Most of the expositions were planned so lavishly that they ended with large deficits, and the Pan-American of 1901 at Buffalo, New York, was rocked by the horror of President McKinley's assassination on the Fair Grounds; the fair never recovered from this shock.

Thus have fairs been developing over the centuries, ever spiraling upward, each vying to excel former ones, until the pinnacle was attained in the Universal Exposition of 1904. In the judgment of many persons, no other fair has ever reached the sublime and majestic proportions of the St. Louis Fair.

Because of the proliferation of international expositions during the first half of the twentieth century, an International Association was formed to curb such excesses. Each nation is now permitted only one international exposition every ten years. Since, for the United States, Seattle won this desired prize in 1962, the New York fair in 1964 was not international. Although the United States has received approval for an international bicentennial exposition in 1976, at this point it appears that such a fair will not occur, and therefore the United States cannot have another one before 1986. Canada's Expo '67 and Japan's Expo '71 were both of the international variety.

There will always be fairs and expositions. They stimulate trade and technical advances; they provide a sense of achievement in their granting of awards for excellence; and the merry-making answers one of man's deepest needs as he gropes his way through a lifetime of work.

And there are always strollers at every fair, seeking both pleasure and enlightenment.

Official World's Fair Flag: Fleur-de-lis and stars of gold on a field of blue; red, white and yellow stripes of equal width.

Margaret Johanson Witherspoon

Margaret Johanson Witherspoon has been an almost lifetime resident of St. Louis. She attended the local public schools, was an honor graduate of Queens College, Charlotte, North Carolina, engaged in graduate studies at three universities, and devoted several years to teaching in the St. Louis County schools. The mother of three children, she is married to William Witherspoon, native St. Louis business man.

Her interest in the Fair stems from stories told to her by her parents who visited the Fair on their wedding trip, and also by the fact that many of her childhood leisure hours were spent in the Fair area of Forest Park. Her keen appreciation of the relics, traditions and historical buildings of the city voices an urgent hope that their worth may be recognized with a vigorous program of preservation.

Although a teacher during most of her lifetime, Frances Johanson Krebs has always been an artist. She attended the St. Louis School of Fine Arts, was graduated as the valedictorian of her class from Queens College, Charlotte, North Carolina, studied in France and travelled widely until she married William Krebs and settled in St. Louis. Among other things, Mrs. Krebs is known for her miniature mosaics made with postage stamps and has exhibited at the St. Louis Art Museum. She is also a poet, several of her poems having been published in anthologies and periodicals.

After widowhood of thirteen years Frances married, in October 1978, Allen A. Fain of Hayward, California, whom she met while teaching at the School of the Ozarks, Point Lookout, Mo. fifty years ago.

Frances Johanson Krebs Fain

Elinor Martineau Coyle

Well known for her frequent lectures, television and radio appearances discussing historical aspects of St. Louis (especially its heritage homes); her tours to historic areas of the community; and the photographer and author of three photographic histories of St. Louis (*Old St. Louis Homes*: *The Stories They Tell; St. Louis*: *Portrait Of A River City* and *St. Louis Homes 1866-1916: The Golden Age*) which have traveled the world as ambassadors for the city, Elinor Martineau Coyle has earned the sobriquet of "St. Louis' explorer in residence."

A graduate of the University of Wisconsin magna cum laude, in private life she is the wife of Charles S. Coyle, St. Louis business man.

China's official pavilion at the Fair was a copy of the summer palace of Prince Pu Lun. Chinese artisans directed the American carpenters who constructed the framework. More than six thousand pieces of wood and embellishment were installed. Several structures united by a wall comprised the palace, in the center of which was an open court with garden, pagoda and goldfish pond. Entrance to the court was through a high gate and in front of the pavilion was a pagoda, gorgeous in scarlet, gold and blue.